FIRST Robotics

CHERRY LAKE PUBLISHING • ANN ARBOR, MICHIGAN

by Nancy Benovich Gilby

CHERRY LAKE Publishing

A Note to Adults: Please review the instructions for the activities in this book before allowing children to do them. Be sure to help them with any activities you do not think they can safely complete on their own.

A Note to Kids: Be sure to ask an adult for help with these activities when you need it. Always put your safety first!

Published in the United States of America by Cherry Lake Publishing
Ann Arbor, Michigan
www.cherrylakepublishing.com

Series Editor: Kristin Fontichiaro
Photo Credits: Cover and page 1, The Bakken Museum/tinyurl.com/ppn4vga/CC-BY-SA-2.0; page 4, NASA Kennedy/tinyurl.com/m42phqe/CC-BY-SA-2.0; page 6, Adam/tinyurl.com/k4sl-sjm/CC-BY-SA-2.0; page 7, Curtis McHale/tinyurl.com/m66kk9r/CC-BY-SA-2.0; pages 8 and 24, Kristin Fontichiaro; page 9, N A I T/tinyurl.com/mbcut7v/CC-BY-ND-2.0; page 11, Priit Tammets/tinyurl.com/n6a8hth/CC-BY-2.0; page 13, Terry Robinson/tinyurl.com/n39pwuk/CC-BY-SA-2.0; page 14, thomas_sly/tinyurl.com/mftudfz/CC-BY-2.0; page 15, Fortune Live Media/tinyurl.com/maquzaq/CC-BY-ND-2.0; page 18, North Charleston/tinyurl.com/mtdt4uf/CC-BY-SA-2.0; page 19, Nic McPhee/tinyurl.com/kp2temu/CC-BY-SA-2.0; page 21, North Charleston/tinyurl.com/n8pg9fe/CC-BY-SA-2.0; pages 22 and 27, Nancy Benovich Gilby; page 23, Nic McPhee/tinyurl.com/lbz8cqe/CC-BY-SA-2.0; page 25, Hillary/tinyurl.com/nyrnebb/CC-BY-SA-2.0; page 26, North Charleston/tinyurl.com/mmjlxag/CC-BY-SA-2.0; page 28, FRC® Team 836 The RoboBees/tinyurl.com/k88d8h4/CC-BY-2.0

Library of Congress Cataloging-in-Publication Data
Gilby, Nancy Benovich, author.
 FIRST robotics/by Nancy Benovich Gilby.
    pages cm.—(Makers as innovators)
 Audience: Grades 4 to 6.
 Includes bibliographical references and index.
 ISBN 978-1-63362-378-1 (lib. bdg.)—ISBN 978-1-63362-406-1 (pbk.)—ISBN 978-1-63362-434-4 (pdf)—ISBN 978-1-63362-462-7 (e-book) 1. Kamen, Dean—Juvenile literature. 2. FIRST Robotics Competition—Juvenile literature. 3. Robotics—Juvenile literature. 4. Inventions—Juvenile literature. I. Title. II. Title: For Inspiration and Recognition of Science and Technology robotics. III. Series: 21st century skills innovation library. Makers as innovators.
 TJ211.2.G56 2016
 629.8'92—dc23   2015013323

Cherry Lake Publishing would like to acknowledge the work of the Partnership for 21st Century Skills. Please visit www.p21.org for more information.

Printed in the United States of America
Corporate Graphics
July 2015

Contents

Chapter 1

Welcome to FIRST Robotics

magine a huge place like a high school gym. There's cool music playing. Students are all dressed up with wild hair, crazy hats, and colorful T-shirts. Team banners and flags are waving. It's a big, loud event. What's going on?

Then you see it. On the gym floor, two teams are each formed around a table. Between them, there are obstacles out on the floor, and robots are zooming

Teams compete at a 2014 FIRST Robotics event in Florida.

around. Sounds! Movement! Cheering! The clock is running. Two and a half minutes are all these robots get to show their stuff.

The robots come back to home base, a wood-topped table with bumpers along the edges. One of the teams rushes to see what adjustments need to be made. What? The robot is out of batteries? Is the match over?

It's not over yet. What's happening? The other team is coming to help! Have you ever been to a competition where one team helps another? If you haven't, welcome to FIRST Robotics, a robot competition where good sportsmanship is more important than winning. If a part breaks on someone's robot, another team pitches in. Nobody gets left behind in FIRST competitions.

FIRST stands for "For Inspiration and Recognition of Science and Technology." It's a national organization founded by **engineer** and inventor Dean Kamen. You may have heard of some of Kamen's inventions, which include a pump that helps people with diabetes keep their blood sugar in check as well as the Segway scooter.

Engineers love to figure things out, see how things work, and make new projects and inventions. Kamen thought more kids might learn to love science the way he did if they got to build their own robots. You

The Amazing Asimo

Some people say that robots can never act exactly like humans. But Asimo, a robot created by the car manufacturer Honda, has many people thinking twice about that idea. Asimo can walk, talk, carry a tray, climb stairs, dance, and even play soccer! Honda's leadership hopes that in the future, Asimo will be able to help people with special needs. They have even taught Asimo to use American Sign Language so it can communicate with deaf people. Check YouTube to find some videos of this incredible robot in action!

can learn about science from reading books, but what makes it really come alive is when you are part of the scientific community. Anyone who makes their own inventions is part of this community, and robots are some of the most creative inventions you can make! Some robots can move and make noises. Others can lift up objects and spin them around. If you get good enough at building robots, you might even create one that can walk and talk!

Chapter 2

What Is FIRST Robotics?

FIRST Robotics combines the engineering challenge of a robotics competition with real-world problem solving and hands-on inventing. If you like to take things apart and assemble them into something new, FIRST might be your kind of club.

FIRST is divided into three levels for elementary, middle, and high school students. The first level is the Junior FIRST LEGO League, or Junior FLL. This league is

LEGO robotics kits add new excitement to familiar LEGO bricks.

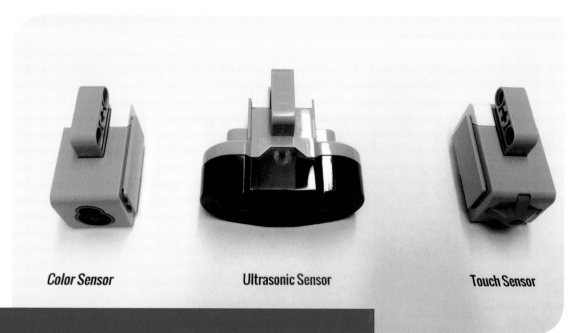

Color Sensor Ultrasonic Sensor Touch Sensor

The LEGO Mindstorms EV3 kits used in FIRST Robotics competitions come with many types of sensors. The color sensor (left) can identify up to eight different colors. The ultrasonic sensor (center) sends out invisible signals that echo back to help the Mindstorms know how far they are from solid objects. The touch sensor (right) has a spring in it that lets the robot know when it is touching something.

for students who are 5 to 8 years old. Junior FLL's competition involves finding a solution to an open-ended problem. An open-ended problem is a challenge for which there could be multiple solutions.

To solve the problem, teams use kits made up of LEGO bricks, motors, and simple sensors to create basic robots. Sensors help a robot measure distance, sound, pressure, or temperature. For example, your thermostat at home has a sensor in it that measures how cold your house is. When it senses that the temperature has gotten too cold, the thermostat's sensor signals the furnace to turn on and produce more heat.

Junior FLL teams also write computer code to create **software** that tells the motors how to move. By combining the **hardware**—the bricks, motors, and sensors—with this software, the team creates a robot solution to the problem. The team makes a poster and a presentation to explain the problem and the solution to the judges. The presentation can take many forms. Some teams even create songs and dances to present their solution and show their enthusiasm for their work.

An FLL team puts its LEGO Mindstorms NXT robot to the test in a competition.

Is FIRST Robotics for You?

FIRST is a team sport, so you're never on your own. You're part of a team of kids. By working with a group of people who have diverse skills and interests, you can learn and accomplish more than you could alone. FIRST teams all have mentors who can help teach them the skills they need to build and program their robots. The mentors make it fun to learn.

If FIRST Robotics sounds like your kind of organization, check out the FIRST Robotics Web site. You'll learn more about the types of teams and projects that are just right for you. You can see photos of past events, watch videos, see which celebrities are FIRST supporters, and volunteer to help out.

Junior FLL students get together with their club once or twice a week for about two months to work on their robots. Then competition day arrives!

The students go before a set of judges to talk about the problem, the group's solution, and how the team went about solving the problem. The judges present awards such as trophies or medals to honor the team's efforts.

The second level of FIRST is FIRST LEGO League, or FLL. This league is for students between 9 and 14 years old. Like Junior FLL, FLL competitions involve finding a solution for an open-ended problem. However, participants must also build a robot

The LEGO Mindstorms EV3 set is used for FIRST Tech Challenge competitions.

that performs **autonomous** missions on a field table measuring 4 feet (1.2 meters) by 8 feet (2.4 m). An autonomous mission is a task the robot must complete by guiding itself around the table. One example might be for a robot to pick up a ball and throw it into a goal.

To program the robot, teams create computer code by dragging and dropping blocks or linking them together to make instructions for the robot's movements. Once you can build and program a robot to throw a soccer ball into a goal, how hard do you think it would be to build one that can chase your dog around and make barking sounds? Wouldn't that be fun!

At the third and highest level of FIRST, which is for students between 14 and 18 years old, there are two competitions. They are the FIRST Tech Challenge (FTC) and the First Robotics Competition (FRC). FTC and FRC teams are responsible for designing, building, and programming their robots to compete against other teams. In these competitions, two or three teams partner together against another group of two or three teams. Each team creates its own robot.

The competition involves various games that the robots play against each other. For example, a robot might need to pick up Frisbees and throw them into a goal. During the game, each robot is controlled by a driver.

The difference between FTC and FRC is based on the type of equipment used to build the robots. FTC teams use the LEGO Mindstorms EV3 and create software using the ROBOTC **programming language**. FRC teams use professional-level equipment and program in the Java, C++, or LabVIEW languages.

Chapter 3

The Founder of FIRST

Dean Kamen is a businessman, engineer, and inventor. He works hard to spread his love of science and technology to other people. In 1989, Kamen founded FIRST Robotics. Though he has created many successful inventions, Kamen believes that FIRST is his greatest accomplishment.

The initial FIRST Robotics Competition (FRC) was held in 1992 with 28 teams in a New Hampshire high

Dean Kamen is known around the world for his remarkable inventions.

Dean Kamen autographs a competitor's shirt at a FIRST event.

school gym. By 2015, 75,000 students on 3,000 teams were participating in FRC. FRC uses the same robotic equipment and programming languages that professional scientists and engineers use. This means the teams end up with real engineering experience they can put on a **resume** or college application.

The high school students in early FIRST competitions had so much fun that their younger friends, sisters, and brothers wanted to join in. In 1998, the FIRST LEGO League (FLL) was launched to meet these demands. The new league was an overwhelming

Musician will.i.am is one of FIRST's most famous supporters.

success. In 2015, close to 300,000 children on 30,000 teams from more than 80 countries participated in FLL!

Have you ever heard of will.i.am? In 2010, this Grammy-winning musician called Dean Kamen to offer his support after seeing a movie about the education system in America. The East Los Angeles neighborhood where will.i.am grew up was featured in the movie as a place that needed help improving its education. Will.i.am saw FIRST Robotics as a perfect solution for education problems in neighborhoods like his in East L.A.

What Will I Learn in FLL?

If you're wondering what you might learn if you joined an FLL team, the answer is: anything you want! You will work on everything from building and programming robots to organizing a team to designing team T-shirts to building a Web site.

No matter what special skill you have or would like to learn, you can find a creative way to apply it to FIRST. That is one of the things that make it so fun. Many teams design and make costumes, flags, and giveaways such as buttons so other teams will remember them. Some even compose music for their project presentations! What special skills would you like to learn?

Will.i.am is helping to transform his old neighborhood by personally supporting FIRST teams there. Dean Kamen calls will.i.am FIRST's most famous supporter and biggest cheerleader. When will.i.am addressed the FIRST Championships in 2013, he said, "The next great superstars of tomorrow are not going to be entertainers or athletes, but innovators and thinkers. I believe that we're entering an era similar to the 1920s, and America is in need of the Edison or Tesla." He also produced a video called "My Robot Is Better Than Your Robot." It features celebrities, FIRST robots, and teams and explains the importance of STEM (science, technology, engineering, and math) education in everyday lives.

Chapter 4

FIRST Robotics Mind-set

Do you like to do different things than other people in your class? Are you sometimes afraid to let the other students know because maybe they will think you are weird? Well, on FIRST teams, weird is normal! It's even a large part of the fun. Many students find their best friends in FIRST because there is so much you can do and everyone must work together. No team ever gets a perfect score, and the only way to get anything done is by relying on team members. No one person can do even a small part of the work for the competition without help.

How is FIRST able to create this kind of environment in competitions around the world? The organization has a set of core values that are more than just words on a Web site. In fact, teams are judged in the competition by how well they follow the core values. These are among the fundamental elements that distinguish FIRST from similar programs.

Working together with teammates is a core part of the FIRST experience.

By practicing the core values, FIRST teams learn that friendly competition can help everyone improve, and that helping one another is the foundation of teamwork.

The FIRST Core Values are:
- We are a team.
- We do the work to find solutions with guidance from our coaches and mentors.
- We know our coaches and mentors don't have all the answers; we learn together.

- We honor the spirit of friendly competition.
- What we discover is more important than what we win.
- We share our experiences with others.
- We display Gracious Professionalism and Coopertition (see sidebar on page 20) in everything we do.
- We have FUN!

Can you think of examples when you played on a team or were in an after-school club where the team demonstrated these values? Did you feel that the environment was both fun and challenging?

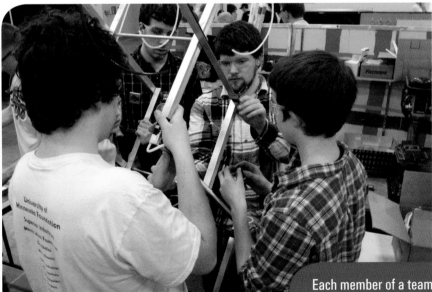

Each member of a team brings unique skills and knowledge that can help the other members.

What Are Gracious Professionalism and Coopertition?

"Gracious professionalism" and "coopertition" are interesting words, but what do they mean? FIRST national advisor Dr. Woodie Flowers came up with the term *gracious professionalism.* It describes a way of doing things that encourages high-quality work while emphasizing the value of others. Gracious professionals compete like crazy, but they also treat one another with respect and kindness. They avoid treating anyone like losers. There is no chest-thumping tough talk in gracious professionalism. Knowledge, competition, and kindness are mixed to create an atmosphere of learning and fun.

Coopertition is all about showing kindness and respect in the face of fierce competition. Teams display coopertition by learning from teammates and mentors. They also practice it by helping other teams at the same time they are competing against them.

Finding or Forming a Team

The best time to find or form a FIRST team is between January and August. This is generally the off-season. You can reach out to the FIRST LEGO League Partner for your area to find out about teams and their events. You can also talk to your school, church group, scout troop, or after-school organization to see if they have an existing team. If not, it could be a great opportunity to start one.

FIRST provides lots of information about starting a new FLL team on its Web site. Existing coaches, mentors, and parents are always ready and willing to help as well. Your FLL Partner can also help with the process. Each team may have up to 10 children with two adult coaches.

To start a team, you need to visit the Start a Team Web page (*www.firstlegoleague.org/challenge /startateam*). The page offers print-friendly materials and videos that help to make the FLL experience understandable. It also offers discounts on the LEGO Mindstorms kits needed to participate.

A Robot Game might involve creating a robot that can shoot hoops like a pro.

Adult coaches can help team members work through difficult problems and learn new things.

New teams can register between May and September. A challenge theme is chosen each spring and announced by May. In early fall, FLL releases the details of the year's challenge. Every challenge is based on real-world scientific topics. Each challenge has two parts: the Robot Game, which is played on the mission field table, and the Challenge Project. Teams participate in the Robot Game by designing, building, and programming their robot to complete missions. The Challenge Project is all about identifying a problem related to the yearly theme and developing a solution to that problem. Past challenge themes have included climate, quality of life for aging populations, and learning.

Chapter 5

The Build Season and the Competition

O nce the challenge details are revealed, teams have 12 weeks before the regional competitions begin. How do new teams get both the Robot Game and the Challenge Project done in that short time? The team members do all the work, but they can

FIRST teams get together regularly to work on their projects and learn new things.

ask any mentor to help them with the "how." Teams find mentors among their parents, teachers, or friends who know about engineering and science and want to help. These experts can help the team learn or go deeper into a problem area.

New teams start by doing the tutorials for building and programming that are included in the LEGO Mindstorms EV3 software. These tutorials walk the team through the basics of robot creation while gradually introducing the more complex use

FIRST Robotics teams use the LEGO Mindstorms EV3 version, shown here. In the past, they used Mindstorms NXT (with orange accent trim), seen elsewhere in this book.

In the moments leading up to competition, teams double-check their work.

of sensors. This means every student can understand robot basics.

Over the 12 weeks, most teams meet two or three times a week for four to six hours. They figure out which missions they will be able to complete. They also decide how they want to build robot attachments (such as arms, baskets, and other pieces) that might help them complete specific missions.

The teams also plan time to work on the Challenge Project by using the scientific method to investigate problems associated with the challenge theme. They start by forming and testing a **hypothesis**. They then brainstorm, design, and build a solution. Most teams find it really fun to select their own problems to work on.

All teams participate in the regional competition. The team that places at the top of the competition—either based on points for the Robot Game or Challenge Project or for special Core Values awards—will be invited to attend a state competition. The top teams at each state competition get to participate in the FIRST World Competition, which is held each year around the last week of April.

FIRST competitions are overflowing with cool things to look at and interesting people to meet.

When the day of the competition arrives, the team will participate and be judged in several sessions. For the Robot Game, the team has 2.5 minutes at the field table to complete as many missions as possible to get as many points as possible. Each team has three tries for the Robot Game. The best score of the three is the one that counts. For the Challenge Project, teams have one try to present their project to a set of judges. Teams also participate in a Robot Design session where they

Judges and coaches watch carefully as teams put their robots to the test.

meet with judges to review some of their favorite missions from the Robot Game, review why they made certain choices about the robot design, and show the judges some of their programs. For Core Values, teams meet with a set of judges to perform a task as a team and give examples of how they use the core values.

The competition starts in the morning and ends in the late afternoon. Teams cheer and dance to support

Are you ready for the excitement of FIRST?

The Right Stuff

To get started in FLL, each new team needs a few supplies. The starting point is the LEGO Mindstorms Education EV3 Core Set. This set includes everything the team needs to build some basic robots. The first step is to create a very basic robot that can be assembled in just a few minutes. The team can then focus on learning programming and using the motors and sensors. Once they have a handle on things, the team might purchase additional sets or materials that allow them to build a wider variety of robots.

one another. Usually there is a master of ceremonies who announces teams while they perform their missions at the field table. Likewise, there is usually fun music playing to keep everyone energized.

The competition ends with the closing ceremony and awards presentation. Teams winning awards all come up, and the judges high-five all the team members. The experience can be stressful when something isn't working, intense when the team works together to fix something, and exciting when a robot is finishing the missions the team worked so hard on. All in all, most teams say it's an experience they will never forget!

Glossary

autonomous (aw-TAH-nuh-mus) able to act independently

engineer (en-juh-NEER) someone who is specially trained to design and build machines or large structures

hardware (HAHRD-wair) computer equipment, such as pieces to build robots

hypothesis (hye-PAH-thi-sis) an idea that could explain how something works but that has to be tested through experiments to be proven right

programming language (PROH-gram-ing LANG-gwij) a language used to give instructions to a computer

resume (REZ-uh-may) a brief list or summary of a person's education, jobs, and achievements

software (SAWFT-wair) computer programs that control the workings of the equipment, or hardware, and direct it to do specific tasks

Find Out More

BOOKS

Benedettelli, Daniele. *The LEGO Mindstorms EV3 Laboratory: Build, Program, and Experiment with Five Wicked Cool Robots!* San Francisco: No Starch Press, 2014.

Valk, Laurens. *The LEGO Mindstorms NXT 2.0 Discovery Book: A Beginner's Guide to Building and Programming Robots.* San Francisco: No Starch Press, 2010.

WEB SITES

FIRST
www.usfirst.org
Check out the official FIRST Web site for more information about participating.

STEMcentric: EV3 Tutorial
www.stemcentric.com/ev3-tutorial
Learn more about using LEGO Mindstorms EV3 to create your own robots.

Index

About the Author

Nancy Benovich Gilby teaches at the University of Michigan School of Information, where she is the Ehrenberg Director of Entrepreneurship. She also coaches a FIRST Robotics team and is a 10-time entrepreneur who now uses robots to make recycled-glass tile mosaics.